LOVE SPOKEN

Germaine Smith

The Center For Healing Press

© 2022 by Germaine Smith. All rights reserved.
ISBN : 978-0-9960421-5-4 (print).
Library of Congress Control Number: 2022905479

All rights reserved. No portion of this publication may be reproduced or transmitted in any form or by any means, electronic or mechanical, including photocopying, recording, or capturing on any information storage and retrieval system, without permission in writing from the publisher, except by a reviewer who may quote brief passages in a critical article or review to be printed in a magazine, newspaper, or electronically transmitted on radio, television, or the Internet.

The Center For Healing Press is the imprint of The Center For Healing, a spirituality center of education or those seeking wholeness.
For reprint permission: germ@thecenterforhealing.us.

Front Cover pictures © Germaine Smith.

For
Emerald Blacksher
whose birth
brought Light to me
&
Colleen Jamieson
who brings Light to everyone

Gratitude to
Connor Blacksher
Mary McPherson
Lois Tschida

LOVE SPOKEN

As a child
    I longed to hear words of Love.
Words that would comfort and sooth me.
Words that would help me realize
    I was valued, important, loved.

Seldom did I hear words
    of tenderness or encouragement.

As an adult, I discovered
    it was not too late
    to hear and say words of Love.

I wrote this book for all of us.
All who—
    no matter what the circumstance—
    want and need to hear Love Spoken

Basil & Sage[1]

---
[1] © Germaine Smith.

WHEN I NEED LOVE

Welcome to the world, Precious One!
The Whole of Existence is thrilled
to cradle you in our arms
as we wrap you in love.

No matter your age,
you are at the advent
of this fantastic adventure we call Life.

You are ready for it!
Be bold and be brave.

Love is the answer to every question.

Love is the foundation to everything we build.

Love is the glue that holds us tight.

Love is the ointment for all wounds.

Love is the quilt that shuts out the cold.

Love is the peace we all seek.

Repeat often
with conviction:

I am loved.
[I love myself
even if it feels like no one else does.]

I am wanted.
I choose me
[especially when I feel abandoned.]

I am important.
The world needs me
[although I am not sure how yet.]

"Where does wisdom come from?
By knowing, dear child,
  that you are a lump of clay,
  you will come to know
    all things are a lump of clay.
They differ only in name and form."[2]

Where does love come from?
By knowing yourself, dear child,
  you will come to know
    all people are just like you.
You differ only in name and form.

---

[2] Eknath Easwaran, *The Upanishads*, 2007, 132.

Love is the only language you need.

Everyone understands love.

I love you.
No matter what.

I accept you.
No matter who you are.

I respect you.
No matter what you do.

I want to know you.
No matter how different we are.

I want you to know you belong.
No matter what.

    Humility   Love   Trust
with yourself   for everyone   in a Higher Power

    Humility   Love   Trust
the only lessons you need to learn

    Humility   Love   Trust
the only assets you need to carry

    Humility   Love   Trust
the only gifts you need to share

Courageous Como Bears[3]

---
[3] © Emily Blacksher.

WHEN I NEED COURAGE

You
will climb
many mountains.
They will test you severely
but they will not defeat you
because you're strong, clever,
resilient, brave & resourceful.

When bad things happen
[and they will]
it feels like
you are drowning.

Feeling sad is okay.
Crying is okay,
Being mad is okay.
Even stomping your foot is okay.

But hurting others is
not okay.
Because they are precious, too.

STOP!
There will be times
when you are wrong.
Admit it. Apologize. Forgive.

CAUTION!
There will be times
when you don't know
the answer.
Accept it. Listen. Learn.

GO!
There will be times
when you move forward.
Embrace it. Enjoy it. Be safe.

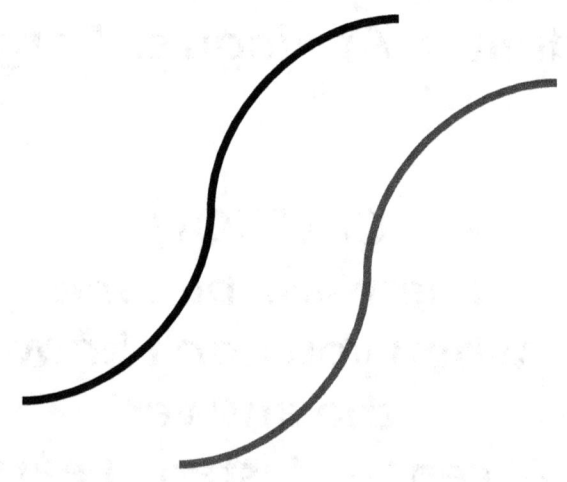

You have a path to walk in this life.

Others may walk with you
    but no one can walk for you.

Some folks may try to persuade you
    to walk their path.
Don't!
This would be a disservice
    to your soul.

All paths are unique.
Other paths may look similar or
    even more attractive than yours.
But those paths are not yours.
You need to walk the path
    that is yours alone.

Know you are:
    courageous enough
    confident enough
    wise enough
      to walk wherever
      your path takes you.

The world is
     a beautiful and harsh place.

When bad things happen
     [and they will]
     be courageous.

The harshness
       —temporarily—
          blocks out the beauty.
Then despair settles in.

Fear grips your soul.
Hopelessness floods your mind.
Panic invades every cell of your body.

That's the time for courage.
Courage to face the harshness,
     to see beyond the pain.

Courage to trust
     that beauty is still present.
And always will be.

In every cell of your body
you are:
brave
courageous
daring
strong
adventuresome
valiant
gritty
and
yes,
indomitable!

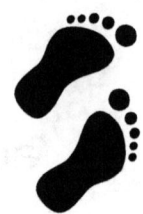

Courage is not the absence of fear.
It's moving forward in the face of fear.

Courage is not standing atop others.
It's standing in your own power
and
inviting others to stand in theirs.

Courage is not talking louder.
It's knowing when to speak
and
when to listen.

Courage is not going to war.
It's seeing the same humanity
in yourself and in your enemy.

Healing Deer[4]

---
[4] © Charlie Brecht.

WHEN I NEED HEALING

You are wounded.
You have been hurt.

1. Be aware.
    Recognize you are wounded.

2. Be honest.
    Acknowledge and own your pain.

3. Be wise.
    Do you need a first aid kit?
        Or an emergency room?

4. Be discerning.
    No EMT needed for a scratch.
    Band aids won't help a bullet hole.

5. Be thorough.
    All wounds need
        physical, emotional,
            mental, and spiritual care.

Healing is possible.

Healing is possible.

Healing is possible.

Healing is possible.

Healing is possible.

Healing is possible.

Healing is possible.

Healing is possible.

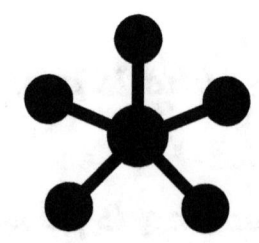

Abuse or trauma is something
  that happened to you.
It is part of you
but not the totality of you.

You can integrate the trauma
  and be stronger because of it.

When bad things happen
  [and they did]
  they don't have to limit you
  or hold you prisoner.

They provide opportunities
  to learn that
  you can
  overcome anything!

Everyone is wounded.
Everyone has been hurt.

That is why we hurt each other.

We mistakenly believe
    that hurting others will fix us
    or at the least,
        make us feel better.

For example,
    if you break my leg
    I mistakenly think that
    breaking someone else's leg
    will fix my broken leg.
I erroneously believe that by
    repeat the violence
    I will feel better.

Healing doesn't work that way.
It only leaves the whole world
    with broken legs.

*Emotions come
in all shapes and sizes.*

*Sometimes they feel
so big and so unruly
and so out of control,
that we question suicide.*

*Keep it a question.
It is never really an answer*[5].

---

[5] Cosgrove, Bloomfield, McWilliam, *How to Survive the Loss of a Love*, 1991, 69.

You are precious.

If someone told you something else,
    they were mistaken.

You are precious.
If someone told you
    that you were only precious
    if you made them happy
or
    if you did something they wanted,
or
    if you looked a certain way,
or
    if you acted a certain way—
    they were mistaken.

You are precious.
No matter who you are or what you do.

You are precious.

Let yourself off the hook.

*You are not responsible for
any abuse you endured
or any violence done to you.*

*You are not blame
for another's mood
or insulting words
or painful strikes.*

*You did not cause any
divorces
or departures
or deaths.*

*Let yourself off the hook.
That hook is not yours.*

Basil the water cat[6]

---

[6] © Germaine Smith.

WHEN I NEED INSPIRATION

BE LIKE BASIL.

I MEAN REALLY,
HOW MANY CATS LIKE WATER?
OR PUT THEIR ENTIRE HEAD
UNDER THE FAUCET?

BE LIKE BASIL!
BE YOURSELF.

[NO MATTER WHAT
THE OTHER CATS SAY]

Hero

[WITH OR WITHOUT A CAPE]

Heroes are essential.

The
most
important
hero
is
you.

Be your own hero.

You are a great artist.

It does not matter
what kind of art you create.

Your creation may be a loving
partnership or a blooming
garden or an inspiring speech
or a beautiful landscape or an
amazing race or a touching
song a welcoming home.

The precious art is
inside of you.
You just need to let it out.

You own a precious body.

You are a body
and your body is you.

It doesn't matter
what your body looks like.

It is wonderful
just the way it is.

Bodies are
marvels of ingenuity.
That makes you
a marvel of ingenuity.

You have a path
    to walk in this life.

Sometimes it will feel
    wonderfully exciting.
You are climbing
    and
    all is well.

Other times you will feel
    desperately hopeless.
You are going backwards
    and
    feel like a failure.

That is the nature of paths.
They zig and zag
    and seldom go straight
        for very long.

You are capable and gifted,
    enterprising and skilled,
    insightful and determined,
    and entirely ready for this.

WHEN NECESSARY
RE-BUILD.

RE-BUILD YOUR DREAMS.
RESURRECT HOPE FROM THE GRAVE.

RE-BUILD YOUR PASSION.
REKINDLE THE FIRE FROM THE ASHES.

RE-BUILD YOUR LIFE.
RE-ROUTE YOUR JOURNEY
FROM ALL DETOURS.

BE WILLING TO RISK.

RISK FACING FEAR.

RISK LETTING GO OF RESENTMENT.

RISK OPENING YOUR HEART.

RISK LOVING YOURSELF.

Herbie the far-sighted goat[7]

---
[7] © Steve Cook and Michele Fallon.

WHEN I NEED PERSPECTIVE

This place we call home is precious:
Earth.

She provides us with
water to splash in, trees to rest under,
clouds to gaze at,
mountains to stand beneath,
dirt to dig in,
stars to dream upon.

She is our Mother
and
we treat Her with respect.

Embrace the paradox.
[That means
opposite things are true.]

We are all very different
& all exactly the same.

People come in all colors
& that color is beautiful.

We are all individuals
& all part of the universal Whole.

You have a very big family -
about 7.9 billion big.

We are all important
because we are all connected.

That means we are responsible
for each other.

It's important to ask for help
& it's important to help others.

It's called interdependence.
[That's a fancy word for "Love".]

There will come a time when
    not only think you are right,
    but know you are right.
You have the correct answer.

Confidence is good
Certainty is dangerous.

As humans, we are limited.
We don't know all the facts
    —definitively
    absolutely—
    to any situation.

Realize there are unknowns.
Embrace the possibility,
    though remote,
    that there are answers
    other than just yours.

Leave the window open
    that there is another solution.

Leave the window open.
Just a bit.

Disagreeing is a healthy exercise.
It helps us strengthen
    our perspective.

Disagreeing provides education.
It teaches us that at times,
    we need to change
        our perspective.

Disagreeing invites compassion.
It reminds us
    everyone is doing
    the best they can.

Bottom line:
    disagreeing is a good thing.

Despite all efforts to
resist, refute, and reject,

everything and everyone
in existence
is filled
with
the Light of Wisdom.

Remember to play!

Playing is essential for all ages.

Play isn't competition.
    It's rewarding relaxation.

Play isn't work.
    It's healing fun.

Play isn't wasting time.
    It's re-gaining balance
        of the body, mind, and soul.

Hopeful Robin's eggs[8]

---
[8] Lois Tschida

WHEN I NEED HOPE

Sometimes you will make mistakes.
That's okay.
You don't have to be perfect.
The important thing is to learn
what your mistakes teach you.

All mistakes
have lessons for you.
Because you are
smart and perceptive,
you will be able to figure out
all your lessons.

Lessons lead to learning
and learning leads to hope.

You will wear many hats
during this lifetime.

Although they all are important,
remember you are not the hats.

They are what you do
not who you are.

Everyone needs help.

Know there are lighthouses
ready and waitng
to assist you
in
setting sail,
navigating,
and
docking.

Learning is precious.

Every day,
learn something new.

The only tool you need is
willingness.

Then discovery is yours.

When the door closes
[and it will]
it is very tempting to
bang on it,
take it off its hinges,
demand by every means possible
that it open.

When the door closes,
be willing to let it close.

Know that what is behind it
is not yours today.
It is not what you need.

Trust that there is another door
waiting to open.

You are amazingly creative.

You can dream it.
You can see it all:
    the parts and the whole.
You can develop each part.
You can connect all the parts.

You can make it reality.

You are amazingly creative.
You can do it.

You belong here.
Your existence is no accident.

You were meant to be here.
Your life has purpose.

This moment is yours.[9]
You are exactly where you need to be.

---

[9] Coach Herb Brooks, USA Olympic Hockey Team, 1980.

Masterful Monarch[10]

---
[10] Lois Tschida

WHEN I NEED JOY

Joy is what I feel
when I see your face.

Joy is what I feel
when you share with me.

Joy is what I feel
knowing our paths crossed.

Joy is what I feel
because you are my friend.

CELEBRATING IS ESSENTIAL

Celebrate weeds.
Celebrate olives and pickles.

Celebrate swing sets.
Celebrate your toes.

Celebrate snuggles.
Celebrate wonder.

Celebrate the smell of pine trees.
Celebrate mystery.

Celebrate naps.
Celebrate open doors.

Celebrate Mondays
[No one ever celebrates them.]

Remember ice cream
likes to celebrate too!

God is the Light;
you are a ray.

God is the Word;
you are a letter.

God is the Forest;
you are a leaf.

God is the Ocean;
you are a drop of water.

May you always be showered with graces.[11]

---
[11] Lois Tschida.

Be content with what you have.

Be grateful for what you've escaped.

Be hungry for self-awareness.

Be joyful at others' success.

Be delighted with your path.

You are worthy.

Not because of
the outside or the externals
but because
within you
dwells
the presence of God.

When you realize this
joy is yours.

You are precious. And always will be. You are loved. And always will be. You are honored. And sacred. And valued. And significant. And wanted. And holy. And seen. And respected. And appreciated. And prized. And blessed. And irreplaceable. And beautiful. And worthy. And vital. And cherished. And exceptional. And significant. And relevant. And priceless And....